S0-BYK-910

5

COPY   31

J
BIOGRAPHY   FULLER, Miriam Morris, 1933-
WHEATLE   Phillis Wheatley, America's first black
           poetess. Illus. by Victor Mays. Garrard
           [1971] 94p. illus. (pt. col.)

           1. Wheatley, Phillis, afterwards Phillis
           Peters, 1753?-1784. 2. Afro-American
           authors. 3. Poets, American.
                                              es 3-5
           ISBN 0-8116-4569-X : 6.48

Livonia Public Library
ALFRED NOBLE BRANCH   Mr83
32901 PLYMOUTH ROAD   66171
Livonia, Michigan 48150

19

Americans All biographies are inspiring life stories about people of all races, creeds, and nationalities who have uniquely contributed to the American way of life. Highlights from each person's story develop his contributions in his special field — whether they be in the arts, industry, human rights, education, science and medicine, or sports.

Specific abilities, character, and accomplishments are emphasized. Often despite great odds, these famous people have attained success in their fields through the good use of ability, determination, and hard work. These fast-moving stories of real people will show the way to better understanding of the ingredients necessary for personal success.

Phillis
Wheatley

AMERICA'S FIRST
BLACK POETESS

by Miriam Morris Fuller

illustrated by Victor Mays

GARRARD PUBLISHING COMPANY
CHAMPAIGN, ILLINOIS

Livonia Public Library
ALFRED NOBLE BRANCH
32901 PLYMOUTH ROAD
Livonia, Michigan 48150

For "Chip" and Foster

Picture credits:

Bostonian Society, Boston, Mass.: p. 21
Fort Ticonderoga Museum: p. 73
Metropolitan Museum of Art, Gift of Mrs. Russell Sage, 1910: p. 43
Pennsylvania Academy of the Fine Arts: p. 64
Schomburg Collection, New York Public Library: p. 34
The Henry Francis duPont Winterthur Museum, Winterthur, Delaware: p. 56
Yale University Art Gallery: p. 59

Copyright © 1971 by Miriam Morris Fuller

All rights reserved. Manufactured in the U.S.A.

Standard Book Number: 8116–4569–X

Library of Congress Catalog Card Number: 77–154858

3 9082 04994954 1

Contents

1. A Child Is Sold

"Here! Here!" shouted a man. "Slaves for sale."

The man was an auctioneer, and he held the arm of a small African girl.

"Look at this fine savage," he continued. "Who will bid for her first?"

The thin child stood on a big block of wood. Heavy chains were on her ankles, and for clothing, she wore only a piece of carpet tied at the waist.

On this hot June day in 1761, the streets of Boston were filled with people.

It was market day, and everywhere merchants were selling their goods.

John Wheatley, a well-dressed tailor, stood watching the slave auction. He had come to the square to buy a young slave girl for his wife. He wanted someone who would be company for her as well as a servant.

The child being sold looked terribly afraid and helpless. She appeared to be so sickly that no one had any interest in making a high bid for her. Mr. Wheatley felt sorry for the little girl and outbid all the other buyers.

He paid the auctioneer a small sum of money and said angrily, "Take off those chains."

Very slowly the frail, fearful child looked up into the face of the tall man with the long, white wig. Mr. Wheatley

8

understood her fear and smiled. "Come, child," he said, taking her gently by the arm. "I know some people who will be surprised to see you."

The child went meekly with him to the carriage standing near the slave market. Black Prince, the young driver, opened the carriage door. He greeted his master and smiled broadly at the young slave girl. The little girl only stared at the black man, who was dressed in breeches and a long coat and wore a white bob wig.

After they had ridden a short distance, the carriage stopped in front of a large, two-story house. A tall pine tree stood at one side of it, and bright patches of yellow daisies grew close to the front steps.

Mary, the Wheatleys' fifteen-year-old

daughter, pushed open the front door and bounded down the steps. Two blonde braids danced on her shoulders, and her full calico dress bounced as she ran.

"Father, father," she shouted breathlessly. "What did you bring me?"

Nathaniel, Mary's dark-haired twin, came running across the lawn. He was dressed exactly like his father in stockings, knee breeches, waistcoat, and ruffled shirt.

"I have a surprise," Mr. Wheatley said, turning toward the carriage. "Bring her out, Prince."

Black Prince stepped to the carriage and gently lifted the little girl out onto the lawn.

"Father, who is she?" Nathaniel asked in surprise.

"She was taken from a slave ship that

arrived from Senegal today. I bought her as a servant for your mother."

Wide-eyed with fear, the trembling child looked from one to the other. Then she stepped closer to Black Prince.

Mary took the girl's hand and slowly led her into the house, saying, "Well, let's show her to mother. She's in the parlor."

As the children walked into the sunny room, Susannah Wheatley looked up in amazement. Her heart filled with pity as she looked at the child.

Mrs. Wheatley thought of the horrible tales she had heard of how slaves were brought to America against their will. She imagined that the thin, frightened child standing before her had been chained to another slave and crowded into a dark, airless hole of a ship for the long, miserable journey to America.

"How old is she?" Mary wanted to know.

"About seven or eight, I'd say," replied her mother. "And now she must be given a name." She thought for a moment. "I know a name—it's Phillis. We'll call her Phillis."

"Phillis," repeated Mary softly. "Phillis Wheatley. I like that name, mother."

So, all in one day, the little girl kidnapped from Senegal, West Africa had gotten a new home and a new name.

Aunt Sukey was an old slave who had been with the Wheatleys for many years. She was surprised when Black Prince told her about Phillis. When Mary brought the little African girl into the kitchen, Aunt Sukey held her close for a minute.

Phillis put her arms tightly around her and felt secure in her embrace.

Lima, the cook, rushed into the kitchen. "Well, bless my soul!" she said, shaking her head. She stepped close to Phillis and took her small face in her large rough hands. "You need some fattening up, little one. I'll soon fix that."

Mary began teaching Phillis simple English words the very next day. Sometimes they worked outside under the trees in the apple orchard, but most of the time they studied in Mary's room.

During the first lesson Mary tried to explain to Phillis the names of the everyday things about her—"chair," "table," "bed." She soon learned that Phillis was a bright and alert little girl.

There were times when Nathaniel drilled Phillis in Latin and elementary science. He worked so hard with her that Mary complained, "You are pushing her too hard, Nat. She can't learn everything in one day."

There were other kinds of learning too. As a servant Phillis had to be taught the daily household chores. For, although her main task was caring for Mrs. Wheatley, she sometimes helped Lima in the kitchen, or Aunt Sukey with the housecleaning and daily chores.

One day after Phillis had been with the Wheatleys for a few years, Mary rushed out to the front lawn where her mother sat reading. "Mother," she shouted. "Mother, listen. I want to read something to you."

Mary began to read from a piece of paper she held in her hand: "Today I saw the morning glories wake. Of all the flowers in the garden, they are my dearest . . ."

When Mary stopped reading, Mrs. Wheatley said, "Wherever did you find such a lovely piece?"

"Phillis wrote it. Isn't it beautiful?"

"Yes," her mother answered thoughtfully. "It is beautiful. God has given Phillis a beautiful mind."

2. Phillis Writes a Poem

Phillis was now about thirteen years old. She looked quite different from the half-starved, frightened little girl who first came to the Wheatley household. Although she was not very tall or very large, she was healthy. Her brown eyes were big and bright, and her dark complexion was as smooth as a chestnut shell.

A little before daylight one Sunday morning in May 1766, a strange event took place in Boston. The townsfolk were still asleep. Only the birds were awake and chirping their May songs.

18

On this special morning, Phillis was awakened from a sound sleep. She sat up in bed. "All the bells in Boston must be ringing," thought Phillis, a little afraid.

She hopped out of bed and hurried to the door that separated her room from Mary's. She knocked lightly.

"Miss Mary! Miss Mary!" she called as loudly as she dared without awakening the entire household.

Very soon a sleepy young lady dressed in a pale yellow robe stood in the doorway. Mary was now twenty years old and extremely pretty.

"The bells," Phillis whispered. "Do you hear the bells?"

Mary nodded. "Come," she said. "Let's look out of the window."

They went to the open window, pulled back the curtain, and looked down the hill.

"Look," said Mary, pointing directly below. "I see father, Nathaniel, and Black Prince. Let's ask them what's happening."

Mary and Phillis hurried outside in time to hear the town crier as he came riding up King Street on horseback.

"The Stamp Act is dead! The Stamp Act is dead!" he announced. "Long live the king!"

"Long live the king," Mr. Wheatley echoed as the crier galloped by.

Later Phillis and Mary sat at the bedroom window and watched the excited people crowding into the street.

"I do not understand, Miss Mary," Phillis spoke timidly. "What is the Stamp Act? Why is everyone so happy?"

Mary smiled. She always enjoyed explaining things to Phillis. "The king and Parliament in England make the laws for

King Street, where the Wheatley family lived, was one of the busiest and most important streets in Boston.

us. Several months ago, Parliament passed a law called the Stamp Act. This new law meant that the colonists had to buy special stamps from England to put on all legal papers, newspapers, and books. The colonists thought the law was unfair and let the king know how they felt. In March of this year the king approved Parliament's repeal of the Stamp Act." Her voice rose on a note of triumph.

"Isn't that wonderful," Phillis exclaimed shyly. "The king must be a great man."

Phillis' heart rejoiced with the people of Boston, and she wanted to express her joy too.

One evening when she was alone in her room, she found a way. Sitting on her bed she picked up a quill from a small bedside table. Phillis thought of King George and all the good things people were saying, and she began to write a poem about him. When she had finished, Phillis, at the age of thirteen, had written her first poem. This is the way it began:

Your subjects hope, dread Sire,
The crown upon your brows
   may flourish long,
And that your arm may in your God
   be strong! . . .

3. A Slave Can't Write Poetry

Phillis sat in her room looking out of the window. She had been sick with a cold during the last weeks of winter and continued to cough.

While Phillis was ill she had time to write more poetry. Because she felt uncomfortable talking with most people, writing had become a way of expressing her deepest feelings.

As Phillis sat gazing out of the window and thinking, a loud knock interrupted her thoughts. Mary burst into the room.

"Phillis, Phillis," cried Mary. "I have the most wonderful news. John has asked me to marry him, and I have accepted." The girls embraced and jumped up and down joyfully.

John Lathrop was a young minister who had moved to Boston. He was well liked by the townspeople, and the Wheatleys thought highly of him.

For the remainder of the day, Phillis kept turning plans over and over in her mind. "What gift can I give Miss Mary?" she asked herself. "What can I give her that she'd really like? I don't have much money."

As the weeks passed, Phillis grew stronger and was able to help more and more with the housework. Lima had died of smallpox the year before. Aunt Sukey had become pitifully feeble, but she and

Phillis did all of the cooking. Phillis en-joyed being with Aunt Sukey, and she watched over her constantly, trying to keep her from doing too much. More than anything, Phillis depended on the old woman's wisdom. She asked Aunt Sukey questions she wouldn't ask anyone else.

"Auntie, will I ever have a wedding?" she inquired softly one day while they worked in the kitchen.

Aunt Sukey sat washing a bowl of strawberries and did not look up. "If the good Lord wills it, child," she replied. "You go on being as sweet as you are, and good things are sure to come your way. Wait on the Lord, honey."

That was the last heart-to-heart talk Phillis and Aunt Sukey had. A few weeks later, Aunt Sukey died. Phillis was deeply grieved. She had lost her dearest friend.

No one could ever take the special place she held in her heart for Aunt Sukey.

Many months later, on a cold crisp day in January, there was nothing but happiness in the Wheatley house. The day of Mary's wedding had arrived.

Before the wedding hour Phillis went upstairs to help Mary get dressed. As Mary stood before the mirror for a last look at herself in her wedding dress, she felt a roll of paper being pressed into her hand.

"It's my wedding gift to you, Miss Mary," Phillis said, shyly placing her hands on Mary's shoulders. "I hope you will be very happy."

Wordlessly Mary unrolled the paper. When she had finished reading, she looked at Phillis through tear-filled eyes.

"Oh, Phillis, it is such a beautiful,

beautiful poem, such a wonderful gift!"
Mary hugged her gratefully.

After the cake was cut and the bride
and groom were preparing to leave, Mrs.
Wheatley told her guests she wanted them
to "hear" the wedding gift Phillis had
given Mary.

Phillis had never read her poems to an
audience before. Her voice trembled as
she began to read. But she gained confidence as she continued, and near the
end, her voice rang out loud and clear.
When she had finished the poem, the
guests clapped thunderously. Some people
were speechless. Others couldn't stop talking about the slave who could write
poetry.

Reading her poem at Mary's wedding
changed Phillis' life. She no longer wrote
for her own enjoyment. When the wife

of a local minister died, Phillis wrote a poem to console him. When Nathaniel Wheatley disappointed his parents by threatening to leave college, she wrote a poem encouraging him to stay. People throughout Boston now began to request poems of her. Very soon Phillis had written a large number of them.

A short time after Mary had settled in her own home across town, she visited her mother to discuss an idea.

"It's such a waste that the world can't read Phillis' poems," she said firmly. "I think we should try to get them published."

Mrs. Wheatley was delighted. "Oh Mary, that's exactly what must be done. Will you look into it as soon as possible?"

The publisher whom Mary went to see gave his opinion bluntly and quickly.

"I don't believe your African servant wrote those poems. It's a known fact that slaves cannot write poetry. They don't have the brains for it."

Perhaps others would have become discouraged by those harsh remarks, but not Mary. She felt the blood rush to her face. "It doesn't matter whether you believe me or not, sir," she said slowly. "But I promise you this—Phillis' poems will be published." She turned and walked haughtily out of the door.

4. Tears of Joy

The winter of 1772 was very long. It seemed as though spring would never come. Warm weather arrived at last, and the earth changed to bright green.

Phillis had been ill most of the winter. She still had a deep bothersome cough when warmer weather came.

"You just need to breathe some fresh country air for a change," Mrs. Wheatley said one day.

Soon afterwards she made arrangements for Phillis to live on a farm during the summer months as a tutor for three children. Phillis enjoyed farm life, but she missed the family in Boston. She wrote often to Mrs. Wheatley and never failed to enclose copies of her new poems.

Meanwhile, in Boston, the Wheatleys and Lathrops were making plans that would soon bring fame to Phillis. At a

Phillis surprised and pleased the Wheatleys by writing poetry.

family meeting they decided that Phillis
needed written proof that she was the
author of her poems.

Mrs. Wheatley said, "We must ask
Governor Hutchinson to call together the
most outstanding men of Boston and have
them test Phillis. If she passes, they could
sign a paper. That should be proof
enough."

Late in August Phillis received a letter
from Mrs. Wheatley asking her to return
home as soon as possible. Shortly after
her arrival Phillis was in Mrs. Wheatley's
room listening to the plans for her future.

"But, mistress," Phillis protested, as she
sat at the head of the bed and brushed
Mrs. Wheatley's long hair, "I couldn't go
before those great men. I just couldn't."

"Yes you can, Phillis—and you will!"
Mrs. Wheatley said firmly. "There are

people who do not believe you wrote those poems, and this is the only way we can prove it."

"But the governor's mansion!" Phillis exclaimed. "What will I say to them?"

"They will ask questions. Just answer them truthfully. Then they will write a paper saying you are the author of your poems. All present will sign it. That's all."

Two weeks later Phillis went with Mr. Wheatley to the governor's mansion. She wore a white bonnet and a full grey dress trimmed with a large white lace collar. Prince proudly drove the carriage through Boston.

Once they were inside the huge mansion, Phillis felt a cold chill come over her. A black servant led them to a room where the governor sat with sixteen of the most noted men of Massachusetts.

Among them were seven clergymen, four government officials, and John Hancock, the statesman who later became a signer of the Declaration of Independence.

The governor stood up and made the proper introductions. "Now gentlemen," he said, "you have the privilege of asking Phillis any question you wish. When all questions have been asked, we will decide what to do."

"Are you a Christian? Have you been baptized?" were the first questions.

Phillis replied that she was a member of Old South Church. Some of the men looked at each other in surprise. It was very rare indeed for a slave to be a member of a Boston church.

More questions followed. She was asked to recite a portion of the Bible, to speak Latin, and finally, to recite one of her

poems. Phillis gave an excellent perform-
ance.

The men talked softly among themselves for a few minutes. It did not take
them long to decide that Phillis was truly
the author of the poems. Governor
Hutchinson asked his aide to draw up a

paper, called an "affidavit," part of which said:

> We, whose names are underwritten, do assure the World that the Poems specified in the following pages, were (as we verily believe) written by Phillis, a young Negro girl, who was but a few years since brought an uncultivated barbarian, from Africa . . .

Eighteen men, including Mr. Wheatley and the governor, signed the affidavit.

At last Mr. Wheatley arose. "For Phillis, my wife, and for myself, I thank you, gentlemen."

"Oh, sirs, thank you, thank you," Phillis said.

"No thanks due," came the reply. "It was the right thing to do."

Phillis couldn't wait to get home and

out of the carriage. She ran up the stairs to Mrs. Wheatley's room.

"Oh, mistress," she sighed, throwing her arms around Mrs. Wheatley's neck, "I am so happy." Then she knelt by Mrs. Wheatley's chair and told her everything that had taken place at the meeting. Afterwards she rushed to her own room. There she fell on her bed and cried for joy.

"Oh, how I wish Aunt Sukey could have lived to have seen this day," thought Phillis. "How happy she would have been!" Phillis was sure that this was the happiest moment of her life.

5. A Slave Becomes a Princess

The big house on King Street was now a lonely place. Lima and Aunt Sukey were gone. Black Prince had joined the militia a short time after the Boston Massacre. This was an incident in which British soldiers had fired into an unruly crowd of Boston citizens, killing five. Mary was living in her own home, and Nathaniel visited only for short periods.

Mr. Wheatley hired a housekeeper, so Phillis still had time for her poetry.

This engraving by Paul Revere depicts the Boston Massacre, an incident that led many Bostonians to join the militia in defense of the colony.

One day in early fall Phillis went marketing. This was a favorite task, but she always dreaded passing the slave auction block. Each time she stood before it, Phillis cried. She could clearly hear the auctioneer's chant, and she could feel the weight of the chains on her ankles.

Several hours later she returned home, rushed into the kitchen, and placed her heavy basket of goods on the table. There was the delightful smell of chicken stewing and bread baking. When she went to warm her hands by the open fire, Phillis found Mrs. Wheatley sitting before the fireplace knitting.

Mrs. Wheatley smiled. "I have a letter that came for you while you were gone. It's from the countess of Huntingdon."

"The countess?" Phillis wondered as she grasped the long roll and untied it.

Some years before, the countess of Huntingdon had invited the Reverend Whitefield—a college friend of Nathaniel's —and his wife to her castle in England. She wanted the young minister to serve as chaplain. The couple had made the voyage, but soon after they had arrived, Reverend Whitefield became ill and died. Nathaniel and the Wheatley family were deeply grieved. Phillis had expressed her sorrow in a poem she dedicated to the young clergyman, and she sent it to the countess.

Phillis read silently a moment before saying, "The countess has had the poem I wrote about Reverend Whitefield published. It will be framed and hung as a memorial."

"Just think, Phillis!" exclaimed Mrs. Wheatley. "At last one of your poems is published. But why did England have to be first? That Boston publisher will regret it when he hears about this. Oh, I can't wait to tell Mary."

"The countess also invites me to visit her," said Phillis.

"Wouldn't that be grand!" exclaimed Mrs. Wheatley.

Phillis nodded. "It's something to dream about."

For the next month Phillis was too sick even to dream. Mrs. Wheatley called the doctor, but several weeks passed before Phillis was herself again.

Mrs. Wheatley could not forget the countess' invitation to Phillis. One spring night she had a long talk with her husband and convinced him that Phillis should make the journey to England.

"After all," she said proudly, "Phillis is a published poetess in England."

Phillis did not want to leave her mistress, but Mrs. Wheatley turned deaf ears to her pleas to stay in Boston.

On a May morning in 1773, the Wheatleys and Phillis took the short ride to Boston harbor. The Lathrops were already waiting at the dock. After sad

farewells, Phillis began the long voyage
across the ocean. This time she wasn't
cast below deck in chains. She sailed as
a passenger. The entire trip was like a
dream—could it be possible that she, a
slave, was going to be a guest in an
English castle?

After many weeks at sea, the ship
finally dropped anchor in Liverpool har-

bor. The countess' coachman met Phillis at the ship. They started the trip to the castle late that evening and arrived as dawn was breaking.

When Phillis saw the huge stone structure topped with towers and turrets, she was overcome with excitement.

"Oh, what beauty," she whispered.

Soon they passed a tall gatehouse, and

Phillis stepped out onto freshly scrubbed cobblestones. She was staring up at the ancient castle when courteous servants rushed out. They ushered her into a high and spacious hall, tastefully decorated with colorful tapestries and dark, heavy furniture. Gazing about in awe, Phillis at first did not notice the countess walking down the staircase to greet her.

"Welcome, Miss Wheatley," the countess said graciously. "Welcome to England."

Phillis curtsied respectfully to her hostess.

"You must be tired after the long trip," the countess said. "I am sure you would like to retire to your room. Breakfast will be served within the hour." She smiled. "I have a small surprise, but it can wait."

At breakfast the countess told Phillis about the surprise. "I learned from Mrs.

Whitefield that the poem you dedicated to her late husband was not the first you had written. She said that you had written many for the townspeople of Boston. I made haste to find a publisher interested in printing a book of your poems."

"Your Grace," Phillis breathed, "how wonderful!"

About a month later the countess gave a garden party in honor of Phillis. Many of the countess' special friends attended. One of the guests at the party was Lord Dartmouth, a former lord mayor of London.

When Phillis' book was finally published that December, it was entitled *Poems on Various Subjects, Religious and Moral.*

The people of London were now aware of the African poetess who was living among them. They began to refer to her fondly as "The Black Poetess." It meant nothing to them that she was an African slave in Boston. In London she became known for what she was—an outstanding writer.

Shortly after Phillis' book was published, Lord Dartmouth gave a lavish party in her honor. Phillis astounded and charmed all the guests with her honest and humble manner. She looked beautiful in a cream-colored gown that complemented her dark skin.

This party was one of many social events that Phillis attended. The countess and Lord Dartmouth decided that she must enjoy the highest honor—that of being presented to the king of England. Then almost as suddenly as Phillis' dream began, it ended. She received a letter from Mary telling her that Mrs. Wheatley was seriously ill.

Phillis hastily made plans to return to Boston. "My mistress is ill, and I must go," she told the countess. "I'll forever be grateful to you for your generosity. You have made me feel just like a princess."

The return trip seemed much too long. When the ship docked, Mary and John Lathrop greeted Phillis with the news that Mrs. Wheatley was feeling much better. But not long after, on March 3, 1774, she became gravely ill and died.

The family was so grief-stricken that Phillis took charge. In her deep sorrow, she thought less and less about her visit to England. The clock in her life had struck twelve, and as in the story of Cinderella, the magic had disappeared. She had ceased being a princess and was once more a slave.

6. A Letter
from George Washington

After Mrs. Wheatley passed away, Mary, John, and their son and daughter moved into the Wheatley house. It was almost like old times for Phillis and Mary, and Mr. Wheatley had little time to be depressed with his grandchildren underfoot.

There was general unrest in Boston. Since the Boston Massacre of 1770, angry colonists had shown their contempt for the British government in a number of incidents.

One of these had taken place in Boston

British troops arrive at Boston harbor
to enforce the Boston Port Bill (detail
of an engraving by Paul Revere).

in 1773 when patriots, in defiance of the British Tea Act, had disguised themselves as Indians and dumped a shipload of tea from England into Boston harbor.

The British government had been so angered by this "Boston Tea Party" that it had passed the Boston Port Bill, which closed the port of Boston to all trade. Additional British soldiers were sent to enforce the new law. No ships were permitted into Boston harbor, and the city was faced with ruin and starvation.

During the winter following Mrs. Wheatley's death, the colonies grew uneasy and began to unite. They organized a Provincial Congress, and when they learned that more British soldiers were due to arrive in Boston, the colonists prepared for war. Guns and ammunition were purchased and stored in the village of

Concord. Somehow the British discovered where the war supplies were hidden and decided to destroy them. They marched to Lexington on their way to Concord and were met by the American rebels. Here the shot was fired that started the Revolutionary War.

Late one June afternoon a loud blast shook Boston. Phillis and Mary were alone with the children. They were huddled together in fear when John and Mr. Wheatley arrived moments later.

"That noise came from Breed's Hill," exclaimed Mr. Wheatley, his voice trembling. "War has come to Boston!"

Later that day they heard that numerous Boston soldiers had lost their lives in the Battle of Bunker Hill, as it came to be known, and hundreds more had been wounded. A call went out for women to

Yale University Art Gallery

A detail of John Trumbull's painting, *Battle of Bunker's Hill*

nurse the wounded soldiers, and Phillis got ready to serve.

"Phillis, I am so afraid for you. Please be careful," Mary begged.

Every building around Boston Common had been taken over for the care of the wounded. As soon as Phillis arrived she was put to work bathing and bandaging wounds. Everywhere there were soldiers moaning in pain. They lay on beds, on bundles of straw, and on the floor. There were not nearly enough nurses, so Phillis labored all night, until she felt her back would break.

"Will this war be in vain?" she asked herself as she worked. "How long can Boston fight against a country as great as England?"

It wasn't until the next morning when the sun rose over the hills that Phillis started her long walk home. She stepped quickly and cautiously through the familiar, crooked streets of Boston. She was nearly home when she heard footsteps behind her.

"Where are you going, miss?" a voice spoke sharply.

Phillis whirled around, fearing that she would face a red-coated British soldier. She was relieved to find instead a young

man dressed in dark clothes and wearing a white wig—and he was black! He told Phillis that he was a soldier, one of the free black men who had joined the Massachusetts militia to help defend the colony. She thought he was the handsomest man she had ever met!

"I am going home," she told him. "I have been nursing the wounded."

"You must hurry along then," said the soldier with great authority.

Phillis took a few steps and then hesitated.

"What will become of Boston now?" she asked quickly.

"I am not worried, miss," the young soldier answered with confidence. "General George Washington and his army have set up headquarters just a few miles away in Cambridge. They will be coming soon."

Mary, who had been looking for Phillis, breathed a sigh of relief when she saw her coming toward the house. She ran to the front door and flung it open. "Thank heavens you're home safely!" she said. "Come into the kitchen and eat."

"I'm too tired to eat. Oh, Miss Mary, it was all so horrible—so much pain, so much blood. All I need is rest. I think I will go up and sleep a while." She saw a look of distress on Mary's face and was sorry she had spoken so bluntly. "But I did bring a bit of good news. I met one of our soldiers on the way home—a black soldier, Miss Mary. He told me that General Washington will come to help us."

A few days before, Washington had been chosen as the commander of the Continental army. He was now Boston's only hope for survival.

Mary ran up the stairs shouting, "John! Father! General Washington is coming! Everything will be all right now."

Phillis went to her room and was asleep the instant her head touched the pillow. When she awakened several hours later, she thought happily of Washington and began writing a poem about him.

When Mary came in later to waken her, she saw the poem. "Phillis, the general

Phillis composed a poem in praise of George Washington and sent it to him at his headquarters in Cambridge.

must see this poem," she said. "It will give him courage."

"I'd be ashamed indeed for such a great general to read this simple poem," declared Phillis.

Mary would not be put off. She talked to John and persuaded him to see that the general got the poem. "You are always talking with the soldiers, dear," she said sweetly. "Surely one of them would see that General Washington received the poem."

John arranged for a soldier to take Phillis' poem to General Washington. Phillis also wrote a note to the general, and the poem was soon on its way.

Days dragged by. Phillis divided her time between home and the hospital.

The winter of 1775-76 was soon upon them. In the spring every able-bodied man joined the army. That left only the women and children to harvest crops. Much was wasted for lack of help, so food became scarce and everyone suffered.

One cold day in February, Phillis sat in the kitchen sewing and watching the day's meal cooking. She heard a knock at the door, and opening it, saw a soldier standing there. She recognized him immediately. He was the same black soldier who had told her that General Washington would soon be coming.

"Miss Wheatley?" he addressed her, bowing stiffly from the waist.

"Yes. Do come in." Phillis stepped back.

Mary came briskly down the stairs. "Phillis, did I hear a knock?" She stopped suddenly, upon seeing the soldier. "Oh," she said, a little surprised.

Phillis started to introduce Mary to the

young soldier, but paused, realizing that she didn't know his name.

"My name is Peters—John Peters," he said with practiced manners. "I will not tarry. I came to deliver this to Miss Wheatley." He placed the letter in Phillis' hand. "It's from the general himself." And he left the women standing there looking at each other in surprise.

Mary and Phillis read the letter together. In it Washington thanked Phillis for the poem, modestly adding that he did not deserve her kind words. He praised her poetical talents and closed with an invitation for her to visit him at his headquarters in Cambridge.

"In the midst of war he takes time to write to me," Phillis whispered.

"And he wants you to visit him," Mary added. "What an honor."

7. "Hail, Happy Day"

The war took a drastic change for the worse. Thousands of soldiers were sent from England to strengthen the British forces in the colonies. General Washington was busy making plans to drive the British out of Boston, but he had to wait until he had enough artillery. Meanwhile the port of Boston remained closed. Merchants became poor and food grew scarce. Mr. Wheatley had to close his shop for lack of customers.

Phillis feared for the welfare of the

family. She could now help scrape together only enough to feed them one small meal a day. She ate less so the children could have more. Everyday Mr. Wheatley killed a chicken. There wasn't enough food for the cow, so she was eaten too. Now the children would not have milk.

"When will General Washington move his troops into Boston and chase the British away?" Mary cried hysterically.

Phillis tried to calm her. "He'll be here, Miss Mary," she said, patting her shoulder. "We can only pray. God will answer our prayers."

Phillis was right. Things did change. In the early days of March 1776, Boston citizens learned that the big guns from Fort Ticonderoga had been dragged overland to the heights above Boston harbor.

The mighty British navy was within range
of Washington's guns. After one unsuc-
cessful attempt to attack the heights, the
British pulled out of Boston and sailed
south to New York. The following day
General Washington entered the city.

The people of Boston ran out into the
streets rejoicing because their city was
free, but General Washington knew the
war was far from over.

Phillis rejoiced too. There was also a new joy in her life. John Peters had received permission from Mr. Wheatley to court Phillis, and now he visited her as often as he could.

"Phillis," Mary said one evening after Peters had left, "I do believe I see love in your eyes."

Phillis blushed. "Now, Miss Mary," she protested. But then she added happily, "He is rather wonderful."

In May 1776 the *Pennsylvania Magazine* was delivered to Phillis. It was dated April 1776. Phillis read it and ran into the garden where Mary was sitting while the children played.

"Miss Mary, a Mr. Thomas Paine has sent me a magazine and in it is my note to General Washington, my poem about him, and the general's reply."

Phillis and Mary were joyful, but Mr. Wheatley and John could not enter wholeheartedly into the excitement. They were awaiting word from Philadelphia, where representatives of all the colonies were gathered to vote. The vote would determine whether the colonies would remain loyal to the king or become free and independent states.

As the days went by, everyone waited with deep foreboding for news from Philadelphia. Finally, on July 5, 1776, the word they had been hoping for arrived.

In the afternoon the town crier rode through the streets of Boston shouting, "The voting is over! Twelve votes for independence—none against!"

The Declaration of Independence had been signed the day before. This meant that the colonists had broken all ties with

Joyous colonists celebrate as the new
Declaration of Independence is read.

England and would now govern themselves. The colonists would have to fight for five more years before England recognized their independence.

General Washington had long since sent the Massachusetts militia home and moved on with the Continental army to help protect New York from the British. John Peters, who had remained in Boston, visited Phillis often, but still the year passed slowly.

Phillis, Mary, and John toiled long, hard hours planting and preserving food and storing fuel. The children were frail, but lively. Mr. Wheatley was growing old and weak, but he worked late into the night making clothes for the family and uniforms for the soldiers.

Very soon the winter of 1777-78 was upon them, and it was bitterly cold. Mary was ill most of the time, and Phillis' health was weakened by a hacking cough. Mr. Wheatley was failing also. When March came with its budding splendor, he died quietly in his sleep.

After the funeral Mary rested while Phillis put the children to bed for their naps. Soon afterwards Phillis stopped by Mary's room to see if she needed anything. "Phillis, I am so worried," Mary said weakly. "What will we do now? Father had so many debts that the house must be sold to pay them. John said that we'll have to move in with members of his church until we can afford to get another home."

Phillis held Mary close as she would a child. "Now, now. Don't cry. All is not lost."

John Peters visited Phillis the next day.

He sat beside her at the kitchen table while she sorted dried beans.

John was silent a moment. Then he grasped Phillis gently by the shoulders. "Phillis, I'm trying to start a small grocery business. I don't have enough money to take care of such a fine person as you, but I just have to ask you. Will you marry me?"

"Yes, John," whispered Phillis joyously.

Soon afterwards Phillis and John were wed in the Wheatley's apple orchard. Phillis was radiant in the beautiful cream-colored gown she had worn in England. Reverend Lathrop officiated.

The young couple went to live in a small room at the back of the grocery store on Queen Street. Phillis enjoyed her little home and loved taking care of her husband, whom she adored.

For a month or two they were happy, but then one day a messenger arrived at the Peters' store with sad news.

"Mrs. Lathrop is terribly ill and wants to see you," he told Phillis.

Phillis hurried to Mary's bedside and took care of her as well as she could, but Mary passed away a short time later.

With heavy heart Phillis returned to her husband. She had seen him only on weekends for the last two months and could hardly wait to be a housewife again.

"Oh Phillis, Phillis," John said when he saw her enter the store. "We have lost the store and I owe so much money. What will we do?"

Phillis looked around the empty store. Then she smiled courageously at her husband. "You will find something to do, dear. We'll get along somehow."

They packed their few belongings and traveled from town to town, looking for work. At last John found a job at a dairy farm in Wilmington, Massachusetts. He and Phillis had to live in an old barn that winter. Here, some months later, their son was born.

"We'll call him Johnny," said Phillis. "Isn't he a fine boy, John?"

John was proud of his son, but he was worried. Now he had three mouths to feed and his job would soon end.

When Phillis could travel, they moved back to Boston. John rented a small two-room shack in an alley. It seemed that most of the people in that neighborhood were either hungry or ill.

The war had now shifted to the southern colonies, but Boston was still a depressed city. Fewer ships sailed into

Boston harbor, many shops remained closed, and jobs were hard to find. John finally got work as a baker.

"At least we'll eat bread for a while," he told his wife, trying to force a cheerfulness he did not feel.

Years crept by and they were hard ones for the Peters. Then, on October 19, 1781 good news rang out. The war had ended and independence had been won.

Phillis was so moved by the news that she did something she hadn't done in a long time. She wrote a poem, which began:

> *Hail, happy day, when smiling*
> *like the morn,*
> *Fair Freedom rose New England*
> *to adorn . . .*

8. Hope and Sorrow

John Peters could not rejoice with Phillis. In the few years of their marriage he had lost a number of jobs and his personality had changed. He was still a proud man, but he had become bitter and unhappy.

"The end of the war means nothing, absolutely nothing for the black man," he shouted one day after dinner. "We fought in the war—the first man to die was a black man—but now that the war is over, we are still looked upon as slaves. And I am not a slave, I am a free man."

"John, I know it is hard for you," Phillis said softly.

"Just look at us," he continued angrily. "We are poor, and starving most of the time. Look at Johnny. He's like a skeleton. Phillis, I hate to leave you and Johnny, but the only job I can get now is on a vessel trading in the West Indies."

Phillis was heartbroken, but she didn't let John see her sorrow. "It will be so

lonely without you, dear," she told him, holding him close. "But I know you're doing it for us."

It was a lonely and difficult life for Phillis and her son. Phillis scraped the rocky earth and planted a small garden. Many times she took a basket and picked wild apples and berries and preserved them for the winter months.

One night when Johnny was fast asleep,

Phillis lit a small candle and opened her old trunk. Among her small treasures she found her books of poems. She read and re-read her poetry.

"If I could get another volume published," she whispered into the night, "we might have a little money coming in."

The next morning Phillis went to a Boston publisher who had published a second volume of her poetry shortly after she returned from London. Most of these books had later been destroyed in a fire. The publisher now promised to print a new volume of poems. Suddenly Phillis began to live again. She spent long hours writing—sometimes throughout the night. Months passed and the poems were not published. Finally Phillis heard that the publishing business had failed. For the first time Phillis was terribly afraid. Her food supply was low, and she had no money to buy more. "What can I do?" she prayed. "My child will surely starve. Oh John, John. Hurry home."

Days later John's ship docked in Boston harbor. He rushed home to his family.

"I had hoped to save enough to get us out of this shack," he told his wife, "but I couldn't."

"You have brought money, John. Let's be happy for that. Please don't worry so. You will find another job."

John didn't find another job, and their money dwindled away. At the end of the year a baby girl was born. Phillis named her Susie.

"Now our family is complete," she said.

Then, without warning, tragedy struck. Johnny became seriously ill, and the doctor could not save him. "Disease is going

to wipe out this whole neighborhood if that water isn't kept pure," the doctor declared angrily.

Phillis, who had been strong for so long, was overcome with sorrow. "Johnny was such a good, good boy," she said over and over.

A few weeks later Susie became ill and died as suddenly as Johnny had.

Now Phillis could not be consoled.

John blamed himself for the death of his children and his wife's sorrow. He became despondent, and then frantic. He and Phillis were getting more and more in debt and he could see no way out.

"I'll take any job I can find," he told his bereaved wife. John swallowed his pride and began walking the streets begging for work. He managed to make enough to keep them from starving.

Phillis spent long hours cleaning the little shack and tending a small garden. When memories of Johnny and Susie became unbearable, she walked and walked. Very soon a new baby was born. This precious little life filled the emptiness in Phillis' heart.

"This little one will have a good life if I can just get a decent job," John promised. "Phillis," he confided, "I have always wanted to be somebody—a lawyer maybe. Some years ago I read law. While I'm doing these odd jobs I could borrow some books and study again."

"John, I think that would be wonderful," Phillis replied, with a faith she always had in her husband.

Soon, however, this dream too collapsed. John owed debts on the grocery store dating back many years and had since piled up more. As a result, he was thrown into a debtor's prison.

Phillis tried to be brave when her husband was taken away, but she could not. She held him close and cried. She cried for his failure to be a success, for the two children they had shared and lost, and for fear of the future that lay ahead of her and the baby without John.

Spring came. Summer came. Phillis and her frail baby were barely alive. Relatives of Mrs. Wheatley visited them and found Phillis near death. They cared for them for the remainder of the summer and until Phillis was well again.

In the fall Phillis worked as a scrubwoman at a boardinghouse. Here she lived in a small room with her child.

Winter had always been a bad season for Phillis, and as it drew near, she began

to cough constantly. She barely earned enough to feed the baby, and both of them were cold most of the time.

As Phillis became thinner and weaker, she missed many days of work.

One morning the landlady visited her. "I'm sorry, but you'll have to leave in a week," she said. "You can't work so we'll have to hire someone else, and she will need this room."

Phillis nodded as large tears rolled down her hollow cheeks.

Two days later, on December 5, 1784, Phillis wrapped a shawl around her baby and lay back on her pillow. Holding the infant close in her arms, Phillis Wheatley Peters and her baby died.

Even though this happened long ago, Phillis Wheatley has not been forgotten. Several editions of her poetry have been published. Some poems have been included in textbooks and other collections. The first edition of her poems can now be seen in an exhibit of rare books.

Phillis Wheatley's poetry was not her only contribution to her fellow man. She had also shown love, patience, courage and forbearance. This gentle black poetess elevated her life and spirit above her heritage of slavery and won for herself a permanent place in the hearts of those who came to know her.

Index

94